Process Art:

Painting with Flow and Freedom

A Path Through Creative Expression

David Omidvar

Published by TekArt Media,

under the TekArt Press imprint

www.tekartmedia.com | www.tekartpress.com

Title: *Process Art: Painting with Flow and Freedom*

Subtitle: *A Path Through Creative Expression*

Author: David Omidvar

Written Content: David Omidvar, enhanced with AI assistance

Illustrations, Editing, and Cover Design: Enhancements of AI generated images, book layout, and cover design were completed by David Omidvar using Microsoft Word and Adobe Photoshop.

For rights and licensing inquiries, please visit www.tekartmedia.com or www.tekartpress.com.

First edition, 2025
ISBN: 978-91-990369-2-2

Dedication

For the ones who trust the unknown.

For the artists who care more about the moment than the masterpiece.

For the hands that shake but still reach for the brush.

And for the children (young and grown) who taught me that play is sacred.

To every friend, teacher, and curious soul who nudged me to explore rather than explain...

To the invisible mentors — those who let paint drip, let thoughts wander, and let the process speak.

To my parents — for their quiet encouragement and openness, which gave my creativity the space to unfold freely and meaningfully.

And to the creative spirit — within me and within you — thank you for never demanding perfection, only presence.

This book is a collaboration between intention and improvisation.

Between me... and the process.

Disclaimer

This book is a reflection on personal experience and exploration through Process Art. It is not intended as therapeutic advice or a substitute for professional mental health support. The practices described are offered solely for creative enrichment and personal growth.

All artistic techniques, terms, and reflections are shared in good faith, with deep respect for the many traditions, individuals, and cultures that have contributed to the global evolution of art-making.

The illustrations in this book were generated using AI tools, with all concepts, visual direction, and iterative refinement provided by the author. They serve as visual metaphors and artistic interpretations, not as representations of specific individuals, locations, or real-world events.

I entrust the colors
to expose my memories,
magnify the moment of truth,
and spot my future dreams
on a simple blank canvas.
Then I am free.
- David Omidvar

Contents

About this Book

This book is an invitation.

An invitation to explore art not as a product to be perfected, but as a process to be lived — to experience painting as an act of presence, emotion, intuition, and curiosity. In Process Art, we step away from the pressure to create something beautiful and instead embrace the beauty of creating.

The techniques and illustration examples included here are just a few of the many pathways artists have discovered over time. From dripping paint to pouring with intention, using natural tools, pendulums, tape masks, or even tree branches — each method offers a way to let the process lead, rather than the plan. But this book is not a recipe book. It's a seedbed of ideas. The methods you'll find here are examples — sparks — meant to ignite your own inner exploration.

It is an inspiration book — one that seeks to evoke your creativity and inner talent. A line, a stroke, a drip, or a click of color is not a rule — it's a borderless idea, meant to support your imagination and carry you toward the unseen horizon of satisfaction.

New creative tools and approaches are discovered every day by artists who are willing to play, trust the unknown, and respond to the moment. You are encouraged to do the same. Add to these illustration examples. Bend them. Break them. Invent your own.

In these pages, you'll also find reflections on the mindset behind process art — the emotional layers, the act of letting go, the dance between control and chaos, silence and movement, frustration and joy.

This book is not about teaching you how to make art like someone else. It's about helping you rediscover the art that only you can create.

Let this journey inspire your creativity.
- David Omidvar

Part 1: Foundations of Process Art

"The process is the masterpiece, not the outcome."

What Is Process Art?

Process Art is not about perfect images or impressive results. It's about the quiet, unfolding moment when your hand moves before your mind has fully caught up. It begins not with a vision, but with an action. A stroke. A drop. A decision made in motion.

In traditional art, the artist often works toward a clear goal — something imagined, planned, or sketched in advance. But in Process Art, the focus shifts from outcome to experience. The value lies in the journey itself. You respond to the material, to your mood, to the unexpected. You let the paint guide you, the color surprise you, and the moment decide what comes next.

Mistakes aren't failures; they're part of the discovery. Layers emerge through intuition. Forms evolve from repetition, curiosity, or even frustration. The work becomes a record of choices and changes, a visual history of thought, gesture, and emotion.

Sometimes, the final piece feels unfinished, open-ended, even strange. That's okay. In Process Art, the beauty is not always immediate or explainable. It's alive in the marks, in the textures, in the story of making.

This kind of art invites you to let go of perfectionism and control. It asks you to trust your hands more than your plans. To be present. To explore.

Because sometimes, the art is not what you make — It's what happens to you while you're making it.

Key Values of Process Art

Process Art is more than a method — it's a mindset. At its heart are a few core values that shape not just how the art is made, but how the artist experiences the act of creating.

1. Presence over planning

Process Art invites you to step into the now. Instead of controlling every detail, you allow each step to unfold in real time. You listen to your hands, your emotions, and your materials.

2. Exploration over perfection

This is a space where nothing has to be "right." You experiment, test, and follow your curiosity without worrying about results. The unexpected becomes a gift.

3. Surrender over control

Rather than forcing outcomes, you let the artwork evolve. Mistakes become layers. Accidents become texture. The process itself becomes your guide.

4. Emotion over image

What you feel matters more than what the piece looks like. Your joy, tension, confusion, or calm can all live inside the marks you make.

5. Discovery over repetition

Each process is different. There are no formulas to follow, no fixed techniques. What worked once may not work again — and that's part of the excitement.

These values can feel freeing — and sometimes uncomfortable. Letting go of rules and results means opening to vulnerability. But through this openness, a deeper connection to creativity often emerges.

Process Art teaches us that making art is not about proving something. It's about experiencing something deeply, honestly, and without apology.

Process vs. Product-Oriented Art

In the world of art, we often think about the product — the final image that others will see. Product-oriented art focuses on composition, skill, and presentation. It's the kind of art that's often judged, framed, and praised for how it looks.

Process Art turns this model inside out.

Instead of working toward a polished outcome, the artist in Process Art works toward an experience. The value isn't measured by how impressive the result appears, but by how deeply the artist engaged with the act of creation.

In product-oriented art, the question might be: "Does this look good?"
In process-oriented art, the question becomes: "Did I feel fully alive while making this?"

One approach is not better than the other — they simply serve different purposes. Product-driven art can require discipline, mastery, and vision. Process Art requires presence, openness, and trust. You don't reject quality or beauty in Process Art, but you welcome them as byproducts, not goals.

This difference shifts the pressure. You don't need to create something perfect or meaningful. You're allowed to simply respond, explore, and let the piece unfold. There's room for repetition, randomness, mess, emotion, silence, and surprise.

In Process Art, your hands lead. The artwork is not a display — it's a trace of an internal moment made visible. It's not about what the art becomes. It's about what you become through the art.

A Brief History of Process Art

The term "Process Art" first began to appear in the 1960s, a time when many artists were questioning the meaning and value of traditional art. Influenced by Abstract Expressionism, Minimalism, and emerging countercultural ideas, these artists began to shift their attention from the finished image to the act of creation itself.

One of the early champions of this shift was Robert Morris, who described art as a record of movement and energy. His works used felt, mirrors, and organic materials to explore how form could change over time. Eva Hesse also became a key figure, creating fragile and temporary sculptures using latex, rope, and fiberglass — materials chosen for their unpredictability and impermanence.

Unlike earlier art movements focused on visual harmony or symbolism, Process Art embraced change, decay, repetition, and chance. Artists documented their movements, poured materials, allowed structures to collapse, and even created pieces that were meant to degrade over time.

By the 1970s, Process Art had become part of a larger conversation about authenticity, intention, and presence in artistic practice. Though it never became a mainstream style, its influence quietly shaped contemporary installation, performance, and even therapeutic art.

Today, Process Art continues to inspire artists who want to let go of perfection, embrace spontaneity, and reconnect with the deeper purpose of making art — not to impress, but to experience.

Common Materials and Tools

One of the beautiful aspects of Process Art is that you don't need expensive tools or perfect supplies. In fact, many process-based pieces are made with what's available — what feels right, what reacts in interesting ways, or what invites experimentation.

Here are some of the most common materials and tools used in Process Art:

Surfaces:

- Canvas, cardboard, thick paper, wood panels
- Recycled materials (old boxes, book pages, fabric)

Paints & Media:

- Acrylics, watercolor, gouache
- Inks, pastels, charcoal
- Coffee, clay, wax, latex, glue

Tools:

- Brushes, sponges, palette knives, Sticks, combs, rollers
- Fingers, hands, feet — your body can be a tool
- Spray bottles, syringes, pendulums

Techniques & Supports:

- Tape, stencils, and masking film for layering
- Droppers for precision or chaos
- Objects for stamping, dragging, or pressing
- Heat (hairdryers, heat guns) to melt or shape media

In Process Art, the tools don't define the outcome — they influence the direction. What matters is how you engage with them. You might use a mop as a brush. You might pour instead of paint. You might let gravity make the marks with a pendulum. Materials are not there to be controlled — they are there to be in conversation with you. That conversation is the art.

Materials and Tools

Mindset of the Artist

Process Art doesn't begin with a blank canvas — it begins with a shift in mindset.

Instead of asking, "What should I create?" the process-oriented artist asks, "What will happen if I begin?" The goal is not control, but connection. You're not here to master the materials —you're here to respond to them.

This mindset values curiosity over certainty. It allows for mess, contradiction, and change. You're not seeking a perfect image, but a real moment. The surface becomes a space of discovery, and the act of creating becomes a form of listening.

To enter this state, you must be willing to let go:

- Let go of outcomes
- Let go of comparison
- Let go of needing to explain or justify what you're doing

In this way, Process Art is not just artistic — it's meditative. You slow down. You observe. You act with presence. Some days, the work flows effortlessly. Other days, it resists you. But both are part of the experience.

This approach doesn't require you to be confident. It requires you to be open.

It helps to treat the creative process like a conversation. You apply a layer, then step back and watch. You listen to what the artwork is telling you. Then you respond — not to control it, but to co-create with it.

The mindset of the Process Artist is not about striving. It is about arriving — again and again — in the present moment.

Part 2: Techniques and Playful Experiments

“Art unfolds when we stop trying to control it.”

Melting Crayon Canvas

There is something deeply satisfying about watching color melt and move on its own. In this activity, crayons are transformed — not by precision, but by heat and gravity. This is Process Art in its purest form: vibrant, unpredictable, and alive.

You begin by peeling the paper off old crayons and arranging them along the top edge of a canvas or thick board. There's no need to overthink the colors or pattern. What matters is how you let them go.

Once the crayons are fixed in place — glued, taped, or held with a strip — you apply heat using a hair dryer or heat gun. Slowly, the wax begins to melt. It drips, runs, collides. You tilt the surface and watch the colors stretch and blend in surprising ways.

Each session is different. The heat, the angle, the air, and even your mood affect the result. You might see rivers of color, layers of texture, or shapes that seem to form themselves.

The point is not to control the flow. The point is to respond. Stop when it feels right — or don't. Flip the canvas. Add more. Repeat.

This practice invites surrender. The crayons lose their form. The surface becomes a record of color in motion. And in the end, you're left not with a designed image, but with an artifact of movement and choice.

You didn't just make something. You watched it become.

Dripping & Pouring

One of the most iconic techniques in Process Art is the simple act of letting paint fall.

You don't need to apply paint with a brush — you can pour it, drip it, or let it slide. Each drop becomes a mark of movement, time, and chance. The result is not a picture, but a history of gestures.

Start with liquid paint — acrylics, ink, or even watercolor with extra water added. Use a cup, spoon, or dropper to release the paint from above. You can work vertically on a wall or easel, or flat on the ground. Gravity does the drawing for you.

Try dripping from different heights. Try pouring all at once, then tilting the surface. Use one color, then another. Watch how they meet and push against each other. Sometimes they blend; sometimes they resist.

This technique honors the physical behavior of the material. You'll begin to see how paint moves when you step back and stop forcing it. You become not the designer, but the facilitator of the process.

And when you're done, don't rush to fix or frame it. Let it dry with its own timing. Let the shapes surprise you.

Dripping and pouring is about rhythm, surrender, and being part of something larger than intention. Like rain on glass or rivers over stone — this is nature in dialogue with art.

Pour and Swipe

Pour and Swipe is a thrilling blend of control and chaos. Start by pouring vibrant colors directly onto the canvas — layered, side by side, or in overlapping puddles. Then, using a tool like a piece of plastic, cardboard, or a palette knife, swipe across the surface. The motion drags the top layers over the underlayers, revealing unique streaks, blends, and cells.

This method invites you to play with transparency, flow, and surprises. You can experiment with silicone or pouring mediums to enhance cell creation, or leave it raw and unfiltered. The swiping motion itself becomes expressive — it can be gentle and graceful or aggressive and bold.

There's no need to map out your result. Just respond to the way the colors interact and the textures evolve. Pour and Swipe encourages the artist to step back, breathe, and embrace the unexpected — a metaphor for how life often unfolds when we allow movement and transformation.

String Pull Painting

String Pull Painting brings grace and surprise into the creative process. Dip a length of string or yarn into paint, then gently lay it onto your canvas in loops, swirls, or spirals. Lightly press it down and pull it slowly across the surface. What's left behind is a flowing, floral, or wing-like form that you couldn't have planned in advance.

This technique invites you to engage with chance and rhythm. The way you pull — fast or slow, curved or straight — changes the outcome dramatically. You can use multiple colors, layer several pulls, or combine this technique with others like dripping or pouring.

The string becomes your brush, and its path becomes the art. It teaches surrender. It makes you listen. And it offers the quiet reminder that beauty often emerges not from precise control but from graceful release.

Tape Masking & Reveals

Sometimes in Process Art, what you hide becomes just as important as what you show.

Masking with tape is a playful way to build layers, shapes, and negative space without planning everything in advance. You lay down strips of tape — straight, torn, crisscrossed, curved. Then you paint or mark over the surface freely, without worrying about precision.

The tape becomes a boundary you can forget about — until you remove it.

When the surface is dry, you begin the reveal. You peel back each strip slowly, watching sharp lines emerge from beneath the chaos. It's a moment of contrast, and often, of quiet satisfaction. You've made something with energy, but also clarity.

What makes this technique process-based is not the design — it's the unexpected relationship between the masked and the exposed. The shapes may feel architectural, fractured, or random. You may choose to leave some tape in place, or paint back into the revealed space.

There's no "right" composition. The joy is in watching opposites emerge: Bold vs. soft. Covered vs. open. Order vs. freedom.

Tape masking teaches us that structure and spontaneity are not enemies. They can co-exist beautifully — if we allow them to speak to each other.

The act of revealing becomes its own moment of presence.
A moment when we pause, peel, and witness what was hidden all along.

Layering Brushstrokes

Every brushstroke leaves a mark — not just on the surface, but in time.

In Process Art, layering brushstrokes becomes a way to record energy. It's not about painting a subject. It's about allowing one mark to lead to the next. You begin with one stroke —perhaps bold, perhaps hesitant — and then respond to it with another. The rhythm begins to build.

You don't need to plan what it will become. The canvas becomes a conversation. Each new layer holds the memory of what came before. Some strokes overlap and obscure. Others break through, resisting disappearance. The piece becomes a visual diary of motion, choice, and mood.

Try using brushes of different sizes. Switch between thick paint and thin washes. Add dry brush textures, or even use your fingers. Layer across days or within minutes. Let time itself be one of your tools.

This technique can feel meditative. It slows you down. You watch how gesture evolves and how color interacts across layers. There's no pressure to finish — only to notice.

Sometimes the painting will feel heavy, even messy. Other times, it may feel spacious and clear. Both are valid. Both reflect something real.

Layering brushstrokes teaches patience, response, and the value of trusting what's underneath. Just like in life, what lies below the surface still shapes what we see.

And if you keep going long enough, something always begins to speak.

Pendulum Painting

What happens when you let the paint swing on its own?

Pendulum painting is a process-based technique where you harness the power of gravity and motion to create patterns that feel both mathematical and magical. You, the artist, are not guiding the brush — but setting the conditions for the painting to happen on its own.

To begin, you need a container that can hold liquid paint and has a small hole at the bottom—a plastic cup or bottle works well. Suspend it from a fixed point above your canvas using string or cord. The canvas lies flat beneath the pendulum's path.

Fill the container with thin, flowing paint — acrylic with a pouring medium works well. Then, pull the pendulum back and let it go.

As it swings, paint begins to drip in looping arcs and spirals. Each movement is shaped by physics: speed, length of string, gravity, and momentum. You can't repeat the same pattern twice.

Your role is to prepare, release, and observe.

You can layer different colors in multiple swings. Or shift the canvas slightly between passes. The act becomes a dance between structure and freedom, calculation and surprise.

This method reminds us that Process Art is not just emotional — it can be scientific, playful, and elegant. It invites us to participate in a system we don't fully control.

Here, you don't "paint" the image. You set it in motion, and let the motion paint it for you.

Hands & Natural Tools

Sometimes the most powerful tools are the ones you were born with — your hands, your breath, your movement.

In Process Art, there's no rule that says you need brushes. In fact, using your hands or found natural objects can deepen your connection to the work. It removes the filter between artist and surface. You touch the paint directly. You feel the texture, temperature, resistance.

Start by dipping your fingers into paint and applying it freely. Smear, tap, drag, press. You may notice how your gestures change with your mood. You can feel playful, wild, or gentle. The result is not the goal — the act of making becomes the experience.

You can also experiment with natural tools:

- Leaves as stamps
- Sticks as scratchers
- Feathers as brushes
- Stones as weights or masks
- Bark or flowers to press, blot, or drag

These tools don't offer precision — they offer character. They make marks you could never plan, and each one carries the uniqueness of the natural world.

Working this way connects your art practice with the environment. It reminds you that art isn't always about skill or control. It's about engagement.

The artwork becomes a collaboration — between you, the Earth, and the moment.
It's not just what you apply to the surface.
It's what you allow to happen through touch and trust.

Texture Play

In Process Art, texture is not just a surface quality — it's an invitation to explore depth, contrast, and sensation. You're not just painting — you're building, layering, pressing, scraping. You're letting the surface speak with dimension.

Texture play begins when you stop thinking about flatness. You might add materials like salt, sand, fabric, or paper pulp into your paint. You might use tools like forks, combs, or sponges to drag, poke, and press patterns into the surface. Each action leaves a trace — a kind of visual memory.

Try spreading thick paint with a palette knife or a credit card-like item. Press objects into wet paint and then remove them. Let bits of foil wrinkle or absorbent paper soak in the pigment. Use glue or gel medium to build ridges or soft forms. There is no rule—only response.

Some textures will dry smooth, others will crack. Some will absorb light, others will catch it. Texture adds not only physical interest, but emotional presence. It can feel rough, calm, chaotic, or quiet — all depending on how you interact with the surface.

This method is about trusting your senses. Close your eyes and run your fingers across the work. What story does it tell through feel alone?

Texture Play reminds us that art is not only seen — it is also felt. And in the right hands, a bump, a ripple, or a wrinkle becomes a moment worth keeping.

Pouring with Intention

There is a unique kind of magic in watching paint spread across a surface on its own terms. Fluid painting, or acrylic pouring, turns the canvas into a playground for color, chemistry, and chance. It's one of the most captivating forms of Proccss Art because it's almost entirely about letting go.

To begin, artists prepare a mixture of acrylic paint with pouring medium — often Floetrol or a similar additive. This thins the paint without diluting the color, allowing it to flow smoothly. A few drops of liquid silicone can be added to some colors to create dramatic, bubble-like "cells."

Once your paints are mixed, you can layer them into a single cup (a "dirty pour") or pour each color directly onto the canvas. Then comes the movement. You tilt the canvas, swipe with a tool, or use a hair dryer or heat gun to stretch the paint outward. The surface becomes alive with shifting forms.

You can't force the result. The paint flows where it wants. It reveals shapes that seem cosmic, cellular, or oceanic. Each reaction is different. Each moment is unrepeatable.

In this method, the artist becomes a guide, not a director. You choose the colors. You pour with intention. But the art itself forms through balance, motion, and release.

This is Process Art in liquid form — Color in conversation with gravity, heat, and time.

And every piece becomes a vivid record of surrender.

Color Flow Experiments

Color has its own intelligence. When you let it move freely, it tells stories you didn't expect. In Color Flow Experiments, the focus is on how pigments interact across a surface — how they bleed, blend, resist, or push each other aside.

Start with fluid paint — acrylic thinned with water, watercolor, or ink. Choose a surface that can absorb or hold liquid: thick paper, canvas, even cardboard. Then simply begin.

You might drop color from a brush or let it fall from a pipette. You might tilt the surface, add water to certain areas, or blow through a straw. Watch as colors bloom, reach, and settle. You can guide them with motion — but not with control.

This technique is especially powerful when using only two or three colors. You start to see how they relate: some merge into harmony, others clash into contrast. The result might look like weather patterns, roots, or dreams.

Try layering new colors onto partially dry areas. Or salt the surface to disrupt the pigment. You can introduce textures with cloth, spray mist, or even drops of alcohol. Each tool becomes a way to influence without deciding.

These experiments are not for making pictures. They are for witnessing transformation. There is no failure here — just observation and reaction.

Color Flow teaches us to step back. To let something beyond our thoughts begin to paint. And in that surrender, a new language of emotion and movement appears.

Movement Art

What if your entire body became the brush?

Movement Art is a form of Process Art where the act of making is shaped by your physical gestures — your reach, your rhythm, your breath. The marks on the surface become a record of motion, not intention.

You can begin with a large surface: a roll of paper on the floor, a canvas against a wall, or even a sheet hung outdoors. Use tools with reach — long brushes, sticks, mops — or no tools at all. Let your arms, hands, even your feet apply paint. You are not just painting — you are moving through the painting.

This is not about choreography or performance. It's about letting your motion guide the mark. Try painting with closed eyes. Try responding to music. Try slowing down your breath and noticing how your brushstroke changes. Try painting with both hands at once.

The goal is not to create a balanced composition. The goal is to become present in your own body, and to listen to its natural pace.

This process can be energizing or meditative. It's expressive without being theatrical. It's honest. You may find tension being released, or joy rising unexpectedly. The work becomes a footprint of your movement, your feeling, your presence.

In Movement Art, the canvas is a field. And you are not only the painter — you are the mark-maker, the dancer, the pulse.

Found Object Interactions

Art is not limited to brushes and paint tubes. Sometimes, the most surprising and meaningful marks come from the things around you — objects not designed for art, but invited into the process.

Found Object Interactions is a technique where you use ordinary items — things from your home, nature, or workspace — to apply, press, drag, or shape paint. The goal is not to mimic anything, but to let objects leave their own voice on the surface.

You might dip a kitchen sponge in paint and tap it across the canvas. You might roll a glass jar, drag a comb, stamp a leaf, or print with the sole of an old shoe. Every object has texture, weight, and behavior. Let it speak through color.

This method is playful and endlessly surprising. You can combine tools and techniques:

- Dragging cloth soaked in pigment
- Tapping with cardboard corners
- Stamping bubble wrap, string, or fruit slices
- Scraping with keys or forks
- Pressing natural materials — leaves, bark, shells — into thick paint

The art emerges from your dialogue with the object. You're not telling it what to do. You're responding to what it offers.

Process Art reminds us that meaning isn't only in symbolism — it's in interaction. And when you invite the world around you into your creative act, even the most forgotten object can leave a beautiful trace.

You don't have to buy new tools.

You just have to look at old ones with new eyes.

Part 3: Explorations of the Inner World

"What we feel becomes what we paint."

No-Plan Flow Canvas

This is one of the most honest forms of Process Art: to sit with a blank surface and begin with no plan at all.

The No-Plan Flow Canvas is not about making a statement or testing a technique. It's about allowing the hand, the breath, and the moment to decide. You prepare your surface — canvas, paper, board — and simply start. One mark leads to another. One color suggests the next.

You might begin with a few loose brushstrokes.

Then pause.

Then respond.

You're not building toward an image — you're following a thread of intuition and sensation.

Let the process move like water. Some areas might stay sparse. Others may become dense with layers. You can use tools or not. You can introduce texture or stay minimal. The only rule is: no planning ahead. No sketching. No correcting.

This practice helps silence the inner critic. It removes pressure. It asks you to trust your instincts, even when they feel uncertain. It gives permission to stop halfway, to rotate the canvas, to start again. The piece is a space for presence, not performance.

Sometimes, something beautiful will emerge.

Other times, the canvas will simply hold the trace of a moment.

Either way, it is yours. And it is enough.

Emotion-Based Pulp Forms

Not all art begins with color or canvas. Sometimes it begins with tension in the hands, or a feeling that needs to take shape.

Emotion-Based Pulp Forms is a deeply tactile process that begins with something torn apart—scrap paper, old notes, packaging — and transforms it into something expressive. This isn't traditional sculpture. It's a way of shaping emotion into matter.

You begin by tearing paper into small pieces. Soak them in water until soft, then blend them into a pulp. Strain out some of the water, leaving it damp and moldable — almost like clay. Then, with your hands, start forming. Don't try to make a figure or object. Let the *emotion* guide the shape.

What does sadness feel like in your hands?

What does curiosity want to press into the pulp?

You can squeeze, layer, press, pinch, or leave it soft and collapsed. You may feel like building it up or breaking it apart. There are no expectations — only sensation.

As it dries, the form may crack or shift. Let it. The final piece is not the focus. What matters is the transfer — the moment when what you carried inside became something outside of you.

This practice is calming, grounding, and personal.

It doesn't need to be beautiful. It just needs to be honest.

And sometimes, the most meaningful pieces are the ones no one else understands but you.

Working with Silence & Sound

The atmosphere around you can be part of the artwork.

In Process Art, we often focus on what we touch or see — but what we hear (or don't hear) can also shape the experience. Creating in silence or with sound is not just a background choice. It becomes part of the process itself.

When you paint or explore materials in complete silence, your breath becomes more noticeable. Your gestures slow. You may become more deliberate, more internal. Each movement feels amplified. The work becomes an intimate conversation between hand, surface, and stillness.

Then there's sound — music, rhythm, ambient noise. When you create with music playing, your body responds. Brushstrokes may echo the beat. Colors may shift with emotion. Fast music might lead to sharp marks; slow music might invite soft blending. Even natural sounds — like rain, wind, or distant voices — can affect how and what you paint.

You can also intentionally alternate between silence and sound. Notice how the change influences your pace, pressure, or choices.

This is not about illustrating music or painting silence — it's about using your environment to tune in to the process. The auditory space becomes part of the texture of your attention.

Working with silence and sound is a way to deepen presence.
To let the unseen shape the seen.
To create not just with your hands, but with your whole awareness.

Paint by Feeling

What happens when you let emotion—not image—guide the brush?

Paint by Feeling is a process where you begin with no subject, no object, and no goal other than expressing the mood you're in. You don't try to paint *something* — you let your feeling become the form, the color, the motion.

Start by asking yourself:

What am I feeling right now?

You don't need to label it exactly. Just allow that sensation to flow into the hand. Let the color you choose match the energy inside. Use your brush, fingers, or any tool to move with that feeling. If your hands want to repeat a motion, let them. If they pause, let the stillness be part of the work too.

There's no need to "fix" what appears.

No need to judge if it's beautiful or ugly.

This canvas is a mirror — not of how things look, but of how things *feel.*

You may find yourself layering anger in red, or pressing calm into soft blue washes. You may scratch into thick paint or float pigment gently. There is no pattern, only honesty.

Sometimes, the emotion shifts mid-process. Follow it. Let the painting change with you. The work becomes a journal entry without words — pure presence, recorded in color.

Painting by feeling teaches trust, self-awareness, and release.

It's not for others to understand.

It's for you to *witness yourself* through the act of making.

Letting the Accident Lead

What if the thing you didn't intend is exactly what the artwork needed?

In most forms of art, accidents are seen as problems to fix. But in Process Art, an accident is often the beginning of something *true*. A drip, a tear, a color that went too far — these moments can open up directions we would never have found on purpose.

Letting the accident lead is about seeing disruption not as a failure, but as a fork in the road. When something unexpected happens, don't rush to correct it. Pause. Ask:

What is this trying to show me?

You might find a new shape in a spill. You might choose to echo a mistake elsewhere in the piece, making it intentional. You might even start a new layer that could only exist *because* of the previous flaw.

This technique teaches openness and responsiveness. It mirrors life: sometimes the most powerful changes come from the things we didn't plan.

Working this way builds trust — not just in the process, but in yourself. You realize that you don't need to be in control all the time. You learn to follow, not just lead.

In this space, the artwork becomes more than self-expression — it becomes co-creation between you, the material, and the unknown.

Letting the accident lead is not giving up.

It's waking up — to possibility.

Self-Imposed Limitations

Freedom is essential in Process Art — but sometimes, a little limitation can unlock a deeper kind of creativity.

By setting gentle boundaries before you begin, you create a container where unexpected things can happen. You give your mind fewer choices, which often leads to more surprising outcomes.

Try giving yourself a rule like:

- Only use three colors
- Finish in ten minutes
- Paint without lifting the brush
- Use only found objects
- No color — just black and white
- One hand tied behind your back

At first, these may feel like restrictions. But soon, you'll notice something shift. With less to manage, your attention sharpens. You begin to explore depth instead of options. You start to work with what's *there*, not what you wish was there.

This approach teaches you to listen—to the limitations, to the materials, to your own energy. It quiets perfectionism and invites invention. The more you practice, the more you'll begin to see limitations not as obstacles, but as portals.

It's not about discipline or minimalism. It's about discovering what happens when you narrow the lens.

In Process Art, we often think of letting go of control. But sometimes, setting a simple boundary can offer just enough structure to help you go deeper.

Self-imposed limitations aren't about doing less. They're about revealing more — by daring to do it differently.

One Material Challenge

What if you could only use one thing?

The One Material Challenge is a focused process where you limit yourself to just one medium, tool, or object — and explore it as deeply as possible. It's not about making the best of limited tools — it's about seeing more in what seems like less.

Choose a single material:

- One color of paint
- One type of paper
- One natural object (like foil, cardboard, string, or a feather)
- One tool (a sponge, stick, or even just your hands)

Your task is to explore everything that one material can do. Layer it. Tear it. Bend it. Press it. Drag it. Use it wet or dry. Reuse it in different ways. Let your curiosity guide you — not your expectation.

This practice forces a kind of intimacy. You start to notice subtleties: how pressure changes a mark, how edges behave, how light affects the surface. You move slower, not because you must — but because you're discovering.

The power of this challenge lies in its simplicity. It helps dissolve distraction and invites you to become present with your material — not rushing past it, but sitting *with* it.

And surprisingly, this constraint often leads to bold, expressive results. There is a clarity that comes from restraint. A voice that grows louder when you give it only one note to sing.

The One Material Challenge is not about limitation.

It's about deepening your relationship with the material — and with yourself.

Part 4: Personal Path and Artistic Wisdom

"Your journey is your technique."

My Process, Step by Step – Series One

In this section, you'll find a visual trace of one of my own process-based artworks. It wasn't planned. It wasn't polished. But it was honest.

This piece unfolded through gesture, pause, and material reaction. I didn't know what it would become — I just followed what felt real.

The steps below don't serve as a tutorial. Instead, they are a record of choices — a way to show how emotion, accident, and presence came together over time.

Step 1 – The Whispering Beginning

A gentle yellow gesture sweeps quietly across the canvas, like a thought not yet spoken. The brush moves without direction, guided only by instinct. The surface remains open — soft, uncertain, yet filled with potential. This is the start of something honest.

Step 2 – The Warming Pulse

Color begins to respond — warmer, deeper tones rise into motion. Brushstrokes become fuller, bolder, though still open to pause. Every mark is followed by breath. The energy stirs, but nothing is forced. A quiet rhythm emerges between stillness and action.

Step 3 – The Turning Point

The energy changes — marks overlap more boldly, and direction emerges from the layering. A stronger diagonal movement forms, not from error but from exploration. What began as soft gestures now leans with more confidence. The painting turns, not because of a mistake, but through momentum — an unplanned rhythm finding its own way.

Step 4 – The Living Surface

The painting breathes with texture — layers pressed in with fingers, cloth, and time. Scratches, ridges, and warmth create a tactile presence. It no longer asks to be finished. It simply exists — imperfect, full of process, alive with marks that carry memory.

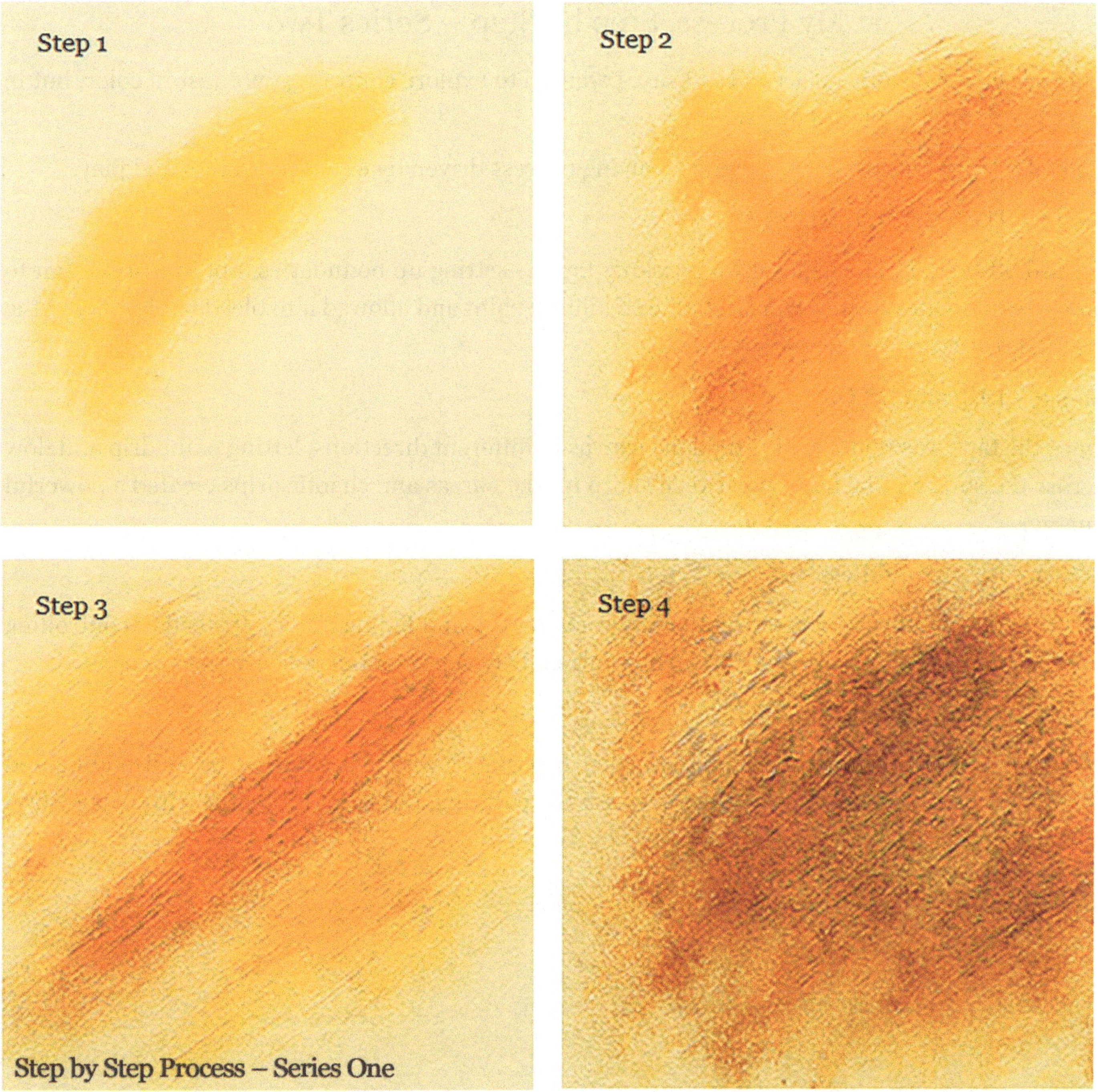

Step by Step Process – Series One

My Process, Step by Step – Series Two

This piece began from a place of curiosity. I wanted to explore contrast — not just in color, but in movement, opacity, and spontaneity.

The following steps document a fluid, evolving process driven by experimentation and play.

Step 1 – The Mask of Intention

I taped off bold, clean shapes using masking tape — setting up boundaries, not to restrict, but to later disrupt. Onto the raw canvas, I poured diluted paint and allowed it to bleed freely around the masked zones.

Step 2 – Drip and Let Go

Once the tape was removed, I turned the canvas in different directions, letting paint drip and flow across the surface. The tension between sharp masked areas and chaotic drips created a powerful energy.

Step 3 – Return and Respond

I returned with a brush, loosely reinforcing certain lines and fading others. Instead of controlling the outcome, I let the piece guide me. The contrast between intention and accident deepened.

Step 4 – Layer and Breathe

Using semi-transparent washes and sponged textures, I softened some areas and highlighted others. Each layer added depth — not to finish the painting, but to let it breathe with tension and balance.

Step by Step Process – Series Two

My Process, Step by Step – Series Three

This painting emerged through play, patience, and a conversation with texture. I focused on letting unlikely tools and layered effects lead the way. The result? A rich surface filled with history, accident, and voice.

Step 1 – Strings and Shadows

I dipped strings into fluid paint and laid them across the canvas, gently dragging or pulling them to create natural, unpredictable lines. Each stroke left a delicate trail — like echoes of motion frozen in time.

Step 2 – Tape, Tear, and Reveal

Using masking tape and torn paper, I created blocked areas that invited contrast. I applied thick brush layers and palette knife textures, then peeled away the masks to reveal surprising shapes beneath the noise.

Step 3 – Found Object Marks

I dipped leaves, sponges, and scraps of cardboard into paint and pressed them onto the surface. These objects left behind broken patterns and layered effects that felt organic and lived-in —like the landscape of emotion.

Step 4 – Pour and Pause

To unify the composition, I poured diluted paint across the canvas and let it settle naturally. I tilted the surface slightly, letting flow happen. No rush — just slow movement. The painting reached a place where it didn't feel "finished," but whole.

Step by Step Process – Series Three

Reflection

Looking back, I don't remember thinking — I remember *feeling*. Each gesture, each layer, each moment felt more like a whisper than a plan. I wasn't trying to control the outcome. I was learning to listen.

They were instinctual, even uncertain. But that's the essence of Process Art: it teaches you to be honest in your movement, present in your mark, and open to the unknown.

In those moments, my brush didn't follow rules. It followed *impulse*. The colors weren't chosen to match — they emerged to express. What unfolded wasn't a vision I had in my head, but a journey I had to trust with my hands.

That's the quiet magic of Process Art: it frees you from the pressure to perform. It invites you to step beyond the boundaries of your thinking mind, and into a space where presence matters more than precision. Where the "mistakes" often become the most honest parts of the painting.

Each page is not a showcase of perfection. It's a trace of something real — a living conversation between intention and accident, between energy and stillness. It's about documenting the process that mattered — to me.

The process mattered.

And in that process, *I mattered too.*

Part 5: Philosophy and Flow

"Let go, listen, and let the canvas speak back."

When Art and Inner Wisdom Dance

Some forms of art come from thought. Others come from observation. But there are rare and powerful moments when art rises from within — quietly, gently, and without force.

This is the space of inner flow.

It's not a technique or a tradition. It's a way of being with your materials, with your emotions, with yourself. It doesn't instruct you how to draw or paint. It invites you to listen — to your hand, your breath, your inner rhythms. It encourages you to trust the energy that moves through you when the mind steps aside.

In this space, painting becomes less about what you're making and more about how you're showing up. Color, shape, and space emerge as symbols of your inner world — beyond language, beyond logic.

The canvas becomes a mirror of presence. The brush a record of intuition.

Some days the work is still and meditative. Other days, it's messy, wild, unresolved. That's okay. Inner flow doesn't require answers — it honors the act of asking.

This kind of art is a companion to Process Art. Both place the journey above the result. Both welcome imperfection as part of the truth. Both recognize the human need to express without judgment.

To create in inner flow is to return — not to a tradition, but to yourself.

Here, your art doesn't have to explain anything.

It only needs to be felt.

My Experience with Intuitive Painting

I didn't begin this journey with a clear plan. I came to the canvas with questions I couldn't quite name — an urge to create, but without knowing how or why. What unfolded was not a method to follow, but a way of connecting with something deeply present and alive inside me.

This approach to intuitive painting invited me to slow down. It didn't ask for results — it asked for honesty. I learned to paint without judgment, to move without expectation, and to trust what emerged. Some paintings felt strange, unfinished, or raw — but they were real. They reflected the energy of that moment, unfiltered.

Instead of rules or steps, I found quiet reminders: to listen to my hand, to pause, to follow the movement rather than forcing it. I stopped trying to control the outcome. I began to experience the act of creating as something sacred — something rooted in presence, not perfection.

This shift affected more than my art. It changed how I approached everything. I observed more gently. I allowed space for uncertainty. I became more curious than critical.

Intuitive painting gave me something I didn't know I needed: Permission.

Permission to explore.

To not know.

To create, simply because I was alive.

That permission stays with me. Not as a set of rules, but as a way of being. A quiet reminder that every time I face a blank canvas, I already carry everything I need.

Freedom from Judgment

The greatest obstacle in making art is not lack of skill.

It's self-judgment.

Before the brush even touches the canvas, a quiet voice often intervenes:
"Is this good enough?"
"What will it look like?"
"Am I doing it right?"

This voice doesn't come from creativity. It comes from comparison, perfectionism, and fear.

Process-oriented art invites us to gently let go of that voice — not by silencing it, but by choosing not to follow it. When you stop trying to prove something through your art, you begin to discover something instead. You begin to move, feel, and respond honestly — without needing a verdict.

In this space, there is no *right* or *wrong*.
No *finished* or *unfinished*.
Only exploration. Only presence.

Each mark becomes lighter.
Each decision becomes freer.

You're not creating for praise or product. You're creating because it brings you into the moment.

This kind of freedom doesn't arrive all at once. Some days the inner critic is louder than others. But each time you return to the canvas with openness instead of judgment, you reclaim a bit more space to breathe — and to be.

In time, art becomes something more than an object.
It becomes a reflection of your human journey — uncertain, alive, evolving.
You don't have to explain your work.
You only need to experience it fully.

Emotion and Spirit in Process Art

When you create without a plan, something deeper begins to surface.

At first, the experience may seem purely physical — color, texture, movement. But as you continue without controlling the outcome, you begin to notice something unexpected: emotion. And behind that emotion, a kind of quiet presence.

Process Art often begins with the body. The sweep of your arm. The drip of color. The pressure of your hand. But as the process unfolds, the mind begins to soften, and something less visible enters — the emotional and even spiritual layers.

These aren't always dramatic. Sometimes it's a subtle shift — a sense of grounding, or a release you didn't know you needed. A color chosen without thought stirs a memory. A gesture echoes a forgotten feeling. Shapes begin to mirror your inner landscape.

This isn't about therapy. It's about truth.
You don't need to explain what's happening. You just need to let it happen.

In these moments, time disappears. The canvas becomes a place of listening, and painting becomes a form of dialogue — between your hands and your heart, your breath and your intuition. You may feel joy, sorrow, stillness, or surprise. All of it belongs.

Some people cry after painting. Others laugh. Many feel a quiet peace they didn't expect.

This is the gift of Process Art:
It connects you to something beyond appearance.
Something honest, wordless, and whole.

Here, art is not decoration.
It is a form of presence. A language of the soul.

Process Art for the Next Generation

In today's fast-moving world, many children grow up believing that art is about skill. That creativity must be impressive, polished, or praised. That mistakes mean failure, and that silence must be filled with noise. But what if we taught something else?

What if we gave the next generation a different kind of permission — not to perform, but to explore? Not to impress, but to express? Process Art offers that permission.

It invites children — and adults — to reconnect with the part of themselves that knows how to play, to wonder, and to follow instinct.

Imagine a classroom where art time begins with a deep breath, not a set of instructions. Where brushes move without needing a plan. Where students are encouraged to experiment, to ask questions, and to be surprised by what shows up. This is not a luxury. It's a necessity.

In an age of overstimulation and self-doubt, we need tools that bring us back to our bodies, our breath, and our own sense of trust.

Process Art teaches:

- Presence over perfection.
- Curiosity over correctness.
- Emotion over outcome.

When children experience art this way, they grow more confident — not just as artists, but as humans. They learn to navigate uncertainty. They learn to listen to themselves. They learn that their inner world matters.

The gift of Process Art is not just what's created on the canvas.
It's what it nurtures within the creator:
Resilience. Self-trust. Joy. This is the kind of creativity the future needs.

Why Process Art Matters Today

We live in a world that celebrates the end result.

Finish the project. Show the product. Make it impressive. Share it fast.

But something is missing in this rush toward perfection. We're forgetting how to simply begin. How to be present. How to create not for show, but for connection.

This is why Process Art matters today — perhaps more than ever.

It gives us permission to slow down. To explore. To not know. It reminds us that meaning doesn't only come from polished outcomes. It comes from how we engage with the act of making.

In a culture of judgment, Process Art offers self-compassion.

In a world of distraction, it offers stillness.

In times of stress or uncertainty, it offers release.

You don't need to be an artist to benefit. Anyone can pick up a brush, drag a color, let something flow. The practice itself becomes a kind of grounding. A way to return to yourself without explanation.

This kind of art also helps us let go.
Let go of control.
Let go of comparison.
Let go of needing to get it "right."

What's left is something more honest. More human.
Not perfect, but real.

Process Art reminds us that we are already enough, as we are.
That art is not separate from life — it *is* life, in motion, one moment at a time.

Art as Meditation

There are many ways to meditate.
Some sit in silence. Others walk slowly, breathe deeply, or chant softly.
But one form of meditation begins not with stillness — but with motion.

That form is art.

When approached without pressure or expectation, the act of creating becomes a meditation in itself. Your attention narrows. The chatter of the mind softens. You lose track of time. You become aware of color, texture, weight. Every movement becomes a moment of presence.

You are not trying to impress. You are simply observing — your thoughts, your hands, your responses. The material becomes your mantra. The surface becomes your cushion.

In this space, mistakes don't exist. There is only the now.
Now this shape. Now this line. Now this choice.

Like traditional meditation, Process Art invites acceptance.
Of what arises. Of what changes. Of what fades.

It doesn't matter what the painting becomes.
What matters is that for a little while, you were completely here.

This kind of practice heals — not through insight, but through experience.
You are no longer outside your life, watching. You are inside it, creating.

Art doesn't have to be about expression. Sometimes, it's just about being.

A pause. A breath. A brushstroke.

A moment of stillness in motion.

The Value of Letting Go

Letting go isn't easy.
We are trained to hold on — to plans, expectations, outcomes, and control.
But creativity often begins where certainty ends.

Process Art teaches us this in the most direct way:
You can't always predict what will happen on the canvas.
Paint may move in unexpected directions.
Colors might mix into something you didn't intend.
A gesture may lead to chaos — or to beauty.

And that's the point.

The practice is not about controlling the outcome.
It's about releasing the need to control.

When you let go, something shifts. You stop resisting change. You become more curious. You begin to work *with* the process instead of against it. Mistakes become discoveries. Surprises become insights.

Letting go in art prepares you to let go in life.
To adapt. To stay open. To accept that not everything has to be polished, planned, or perfect.

It doesn't mean giving up. It means giving in — to the natural flow of creation.

And in doing so, you may find something far more valuable than control: Trust.
In the process.
In the moment.
In yourself.

Because sometimes, the most beautiful work happens when you stop trying to make it beautiful.

When the Art Talks Back

There comes a moment in the process when the art begins to lead.
Not you.
Not your idea.
But the canvas, the brush, the unexpected line — it starts to speak.

You pause.
You tilt your head.
You feel it before you understand it.

This is the magic of Process Art: it becomes a dialogue.

You place a color — then notice what it asks for next.
You move in one direction — then feel pulled in another.
At times, it may feel like the work has its own rhythm, its own voice, even its own will.

This is not fantasy. It's presence. You are no longer "making" art. You are meeting it.

This moment can be playful, mysterious, emotional, or even uncomfortable. Sometimes the painting will challenge you — showing you parts of yourself that are raw, forgotten, or quietly waiting to be seen.

And yet, this is where the deepest work happens.

Not when you control the image, but when you listen to it.

The art becomes a mirror, a whisper, a teacher.
Not always with clear answers, but always with truth.

To reach this space, you must release your grip.
Let the conversation unfold. Let the canvas reply.

Because when the art talks back, it's not just your hand that's moving.
It's your whole being, responding.

Revising Process vs Product

In most creative spaces, there's a silent tension:
What are you making?
What will it look like?
Will it be good enough to share, sell, or frame?

These questions point to one thing — product.
The final result. The outcome. The thing we can show.

But Process Art flips this completely.
It asks different questions:
What are you feeling?
What are you discovering?
What happens when you don't know where it's going?

This is the power of process.

It values the experience over the evidence. It prioritizes engagement over outcome. It allows space for freedom, surprise, and vulnerability.

The product may still come — and it may be beautiful. But it's no longer the goal. It's simply what remains after a moment of deep presence.

When we focus only on product, we often hesitate. We judge, compare, delay, perfect. When we focus on process, we play. We move. We trust.

And something unexpected happens:
When we forget to make something "good", we often make something true.

The world will always reward results.
But our inner life needs something else — a space where making is enough.

Let process be that space.

Art That Doesn't Need to Be Seen

What if no one ever saw your painting?
Would it still matter?

In a world driven by visibility — likes, shares, exhibits — we forget that some of the most powerful art is made in silence. In solitude. For no one but the maker.

Art doesn't have to be seen to be real.

It doesn't have to be praised to be meaningful.
It doesn't need validation to be sacred.

Some paintings are never shown. They live in drawers, journals, attics, or remain layered under new pieces. Yet they carry deep emotion, growth, memory — because they were part of a process that changed the person who made them.

This is a truth that Process Art holds gently: The act of creation is complete in itself.

You don't owe anyone an explanation.
You don't need to turn your art into a performance.
You can create just to reconnect with yourself. To release, explore, or rest.

And that can be enough.

Some of your most important work might never leave your studio.
It might never hang on a wall.
But it will have moved something inside you — and that's the deeper purpose.

To create, not for applause, but for **presence**.

Process as a Way of Life

What if Process Art wasn’t just a method of painting — but a way of living?

What if we approached life the same way we approach an open canvas — with curiosity, responsiveness, and trust in the unfolding?

In art, the process teaches us to accept change, to embrace mistakes, and to stay open to what’s next. It reminds us that control is limited, but creativity is infinite.

And so it is with life.

Not everything needs to be pre-planned or polished.
Not every chapter needs a title.
Not every moment needs a measurable goal.

When you live like an artist in process, you stop needing all the answers.
You begin to respond to what is, rather than chase what should be.
You learn to move with the unknown, not against it.

This doesn't mean living without direction—it means living with fluidity.

Each day becomes a brushstroke.
Each decision, a layer.
Each experience, a color added to your evolving canvas.

You don’t rush to the end.
You learn from the middle.

This shift — from product to process — isn't just artistic.
It's transformational.

Because in the end, the most beautiful masterpiece you’ll ever create is not a painting, but a life lived in full awareness, curiosity, and flow.

The Blank Canvas as Mirror

Every time you face a blank canvas, you are not just confronting a surface — you are meeting yourself.

The emptiness stares back at you.
No lines, no guide, no rules.
Just space — waiting.

And in that moment, the canvas becomes a mirror.

It reflects your mood. Your energy. Your resistance. Your longing.
It doesn't lie. If you're anxious, it shows. If you're open, it flows.

This is why the first stroke is often the hardest.
Not because we don't know what to paint, but because we're afraid of seeing what's inside.

But that's also the gift.

The canvas offers a safe, silent surface to be fully honest.
You can scream in color. You can whisper in texture. You can cry in shape.

There's no judgment. No audience.
Only you, meeting yourself in the rawest form.

Some days the canvas invites play.
Other days, it invites healing.

Either way, it reveals something — not about art, but about *you*.

And every time you return to it, you return a little more aware, a little more courageous, a little more whole.

Because to stand before a blank canvas is to say: I am here. I am willing. I am enough.

What Remains After the Painting Is Done

You've moved the brush. You've layered the colors. You've followed the moment.
And now, the painting is finished.

But is it?

Because long after the surface has dried, something lingers.

Maybe it's a sense of peace.
Maybe a question.
Maybe a quiet pride — or even discomfort.

Whatever it is, it stays with you.

This is the invisible residue of Process Art — the part you can't hang on a wall or capture in a photo.
It's in your body.
It's in your breath.
It's in your way of seeing.

You are different now, even if just a little.
Because you showed up.
You trusted the unknown.
You made space for something real to move through you.

That is what remains.

Not the outcome, but the imprint.
Not the product, but the presence.
Not the painting, but the part of you that was willing to risk, release, and remember.

And so, the painting ends — but the process continues.

Always.

Process Art as a Legacy

What if your most important contribution isn't what you leave behind — but how you lived while creating it?

Legacy is often measured by what endures: works in galleries, books on shelves, names in footnotes. But Process Art offers a different view.

It says: The way you create matters as much as what you create.

If you approached your work with curiosity, if you honored imperfection, if you gave yourself the freedom to explore — that spirit becomes part of your legacy.

Maybe your paintings won't hang in museums. Maybe they'll fade or be lost in time. But the way you showed up in the moment—that stays.

It touches the people who saw you dare, who watched you risk without knowing, who felt inspired not by the product, but by your *presence* in the making.

And if someone picks up a brush because they saw you trust the process — that, too, is legacy.

To leave behind not just a collection of works, but an invitation:

"Come as you are. Begin without fear. Let the process lead."

That may be the most lasting art of all.

Final Reflection: The Artist Within Us All

You may not call yourself an artist.
You may not have a studio, formal training, or a plan.
But somewhere inside you, there is a voice that wants to create.

Not for fame.
Not for perfection.
But for connection — to yourself, to the present, to something beyond words.

Process Art is not about talent. It's about trust.
It's not about being ready. It's about being willing.

To make a mark.
To follow where it leads.
To listen more than you direct.

That is the true artist—not someone who controls, but someone who shows up.

You don't need a masterpiece.
You just need to begin.

To play. To feel. To let go.
To remember that art can be an act of presence, a path toward healing, a practice of freedom.

And that you — yes, you — are allowed to be part of it.

Not someday.
Now.

So take a breath.
Pick up a brush.
And let the process begin.

Part 6: Practicing the Process

"Creativity grows with every experiment."

Practicing the Process

This section isn't about "getting it right."
It's about exploring, trying, feeling, and learning through doing.

Each of the following prompts is designed to help you enter the flow of Process Art—whether you're new to painting or returning with fresh eyes.

There are no rules here.
Use any materials you have.
Take your time.
Repeat exercises as you wish.
Make a mess. Discover what moves you.

Let your hands lead. Let your thoughts quiet. Let the process show you what it knows.

Welcome to the practice.

Exercise 1: The One-Color Journey

Prompt Title: *The One-Color Journey*

Materials:

- One color of paint (any kind),
- One brush,
- One surface (paper, canvas, cardboard).

Instructions:

1. Choose a single color that you feel drawn to right now.
2. Set a timer for 10–15 minutes.
3. Begin painting without any goal. Let your brush move freely — dab, swirl, layer, smear.
4. If thoughts arise, let them pass. Focus only on the sensation of movement and the behavior of the paint.
5. When the time ends, step back. Look not for what it "means," but how it makes you feel.

Reflection Questions:

- What did you notice during the process?
- Did your relationship with the color change?
- Was it difficult or freeing to work without a plan?

The One-Color Journey

Exercise 2: Music Movement Painting

Prompt Title: *Let the Music Move the Brush*

Materials:

- Your favorite music (instrumental or lyrical)
- Paints or inks
- Brushes or other tools (sponges, palette knives, fingers)
- Paper or canvas

Instructions:

1. Choose a piece of music that stirs emotion or energy in you.
2. Start the music and allow your body to feel its rhythm and texture.
3. Begin painting with no idea in mind—only allow your strokes to mirror the music's flow.
    - Fast beats may become splatters or sharp lines.
    - Gentle melodies may turn into soft curves or blended layers.
4. Switch songs if you like — notice how each track changes your gestures.
5. Keep going until the music ends or your energy fades.

Reflection Questions:

- How did your movements shift with the music?
- Did you feel more connected to the sound — or to yourself?
- What did you discover when you stopped trying to control the image?

Music Movement Painting

Exercise 3: Painting with Found Objects

Prompt Title: *Let the World Be Your Brush*

Materials:

- Paints or inks
- Paper or canvas
- Found objects from your home or outdoors (e.g., leaves, forks, cardboard, string, stones, bottle caps)

Instructions:

1. Gather a handful of ordinary or natural objects—anything that catches your eye.
2. Dip each object into paint or use it to spread, stamp, drag, or press paint onto your surface.
3. Don't worry about making shapes — focus on texture, rhythm, and the unexpected.
4. Layer strokes from different objects. Allow mess and mystery.
5. Let the materials guide your hand. Embrace how they behave, even if it's unpredictable.

Reflection Questions:

- Which object surprised you the most?
- Did using unusual tools shift how you felt about the process?
- What patterns or moods emerged?

Painting with Found Objects

Exercise 4: Emotional Color Mapping

Prompt Title: *Painting Your Inner Weather*

Materials:

- A variety of paint colors (or markers, crayons, pastels)
- Paper or canvas
- Optional: brush, sponge, fingers

Instructions:

1. Take a quiet moment to check in with yourself.
   Ask: *How do I feel right now?* Not just one word—try to name layers of emotion.
2. Assign a color to each feeling you notice. For example:
   - Calm = light blue
   - Tension = red
   - Curiosity = yellow
   - Uncertainty = grey
3. Begin placing these colors on the surface. There's no right or wrong—just place them however they want to appear.
   Let the intensity, size, and shape of each area reflect how strongly you feel each emotion.
4. Add layers, textures, or overlaps if needed. Keep checking in with your body and emotions.

Reflection Questions:

- Were you surprised by which feelings surfaced?
- Did mapping emotions visually help you understand or release them?

What would the painting say if it could speak?

Emotional Color Mapping

Exercise 5: The Closed-Eyes Canvas

Prompt Title: *Trusting Without Seeing*

Materials:

- Paint, markers, or any medium that flows
- Paper or canvas
- A quiet space and maybe a timer

Instructions:

1. Prepare your materials. Place your paper or canvas in front of you, and lay out your colors and tools within easy reach. Make sure everything is ready so you can work without opening your eyes.
2. Sit comfortably and take a few deep breaths to center yourself.
3. Close your eyes. Yes — really.
4. With your dominant or non-dominant hand, begin making marks. You might scribble, swirl, tap, or glide your tool.
5. Let your hand respond to what it feels, not what it sees.
6. You can set a timer (e.g., 3–5 minutes) or go until it feels complete.
7. Open your eyes only when you're ready. Then observe without judgment.

Optional Variation: Try the same exercise while listening to soft instrumental music.

Reflection Questions:

- What did you notice about letting go of control?
- Did anything unexpected emerge on the canvas — or in your thoughts?

Would you approach visual art differently after this?

The Closed-Eyes Canvas

Exercise 6: Drip, Splatter, and Let Go

Prompt Title: *Let Gravity and Chaos Join the Process*

Materials:

- Thinned-down acrylics, inks, or fluid paints
- A brush, spoon, or dropper
- Canvas or heavy paper (preferably laid flat)
- Optional: gloves, apron, plastic to protect the space

Instructions:

1. Mix your paint with water or pouring medium to make it more fluid.
2. Load your brush or dropper and begin dripping paint across the surface. Let it fall freely — don't aim for precision.
3. Try flicking or splattering paint from different heights or angles.
4. Let the drips run. Tilt the canvas. Rotate it. Watch the paint move on its own.
5. Add multiple layers over time. Try letting the first layer dry before adding more.

Reflection Questions:

- How did it feel to let go of control in such a physical way?
- What emotions or reactions came up while watching the paint move?
- Does the result say something you didn't expect?

Drip, Splatter, and Let Go

Exercise 7: Using Tape and Layers

Prompt Title: *Reveal by Concealing*

Materials:

- Masking tape or painter's tape
- Paints (any type)
- Brushes or tools for texture
- Canvas or paper

Instructions:

1. Begin by placing tape on your surface — random shapes, straight lines, grids, or curves. These areas will remain untouched until the end.
2. Paint over the entire surface, using bold strokes, textures, or even splatters.
3. Let the first layer dry, then repeat: more tape, more paint.
4. Keep layering. Build depth with different colors and strokes.
5. When finished and dry, slowly remove the tape to reveal the untouched areas beneath. Notice how absence becomes part of the composition.

Reflection Questions:

- What emotions came up while covering and then revealing parts of the artwork?
- How did the process of layering change your relationship with time and patience?

What did the contrast between exposed and hidden areas teach you?

Using Tape and Layers

Exercise 8: Pouring with Intention

Prompt Title: *Fluid Art, Focused Heart*

Materials:

- Acrylic paints
- Pouring medium (e.g., Floetrol)
- Liquid silicone (optional for cells)
- Canvas or wood panel
- Cups, sticks for mixing, gloves, and a flat workspace
- Optional: hairdryer, torch, or palette knife

Instructions:

1. Mix each color in its own cup with pouring medium. Add a few drops of silicone if you want bubbling "cells."
2. Before pouring, set an intention. It could be a word, a mood, or a question. Say it quietly to yourself.
3. Layer colors into one main cup, or pour each separately. Then release them onto the canvas – dirty pour, flip cup, puddle pour—whatever feels right.
4. Tilt the canvas slowly, letting paint flow and blend. Use tools to move the paint—or simply let gravity decide.
5. Watch what emerges without trying to control it. Stay present.

Reflection Questions:

- Did the intention you set shape how you moved or reacted during the process?
- What patterns or surprises emerged?

How did it feel to collaborate with the unpredictability of fluid materials?

Pouring with Intention

Exercise 9: Pendulum Painting

Prompt Title: *Swing, Release, Create*

Materials:

- A plastic cup or small bottle with a hole at the bottom
- String or twine
- Acrylic paint thinned with water or pouring medium
- Canvas or thick paper
- A way to hang the pendulum (e.g., tripod, ceiling hook, broomstick between chairs)

Instructions:

1. Set up your pendulum so it hangs freely above the center of your canvas.
2. Thin your paint so it flows easily. Pour it into the cup, covering the hole with your finger.
3. Let the pendulum swing while you release the paint. Watch how gravity and motion create geometric paths and spirals.
4. Try different lengths of swing, angles, or paint colors. Let one layer dry before adding another if desired.
5. Focus not on the image, but on the rhythm of the swing and the meditative pace of the process.

Reflection Questions:

- How did it feel to create through motion rather than direct control?
- Did the patterns remind you of anything natural or emotional?
- What did you learn about timing, rhythm, or surrender?

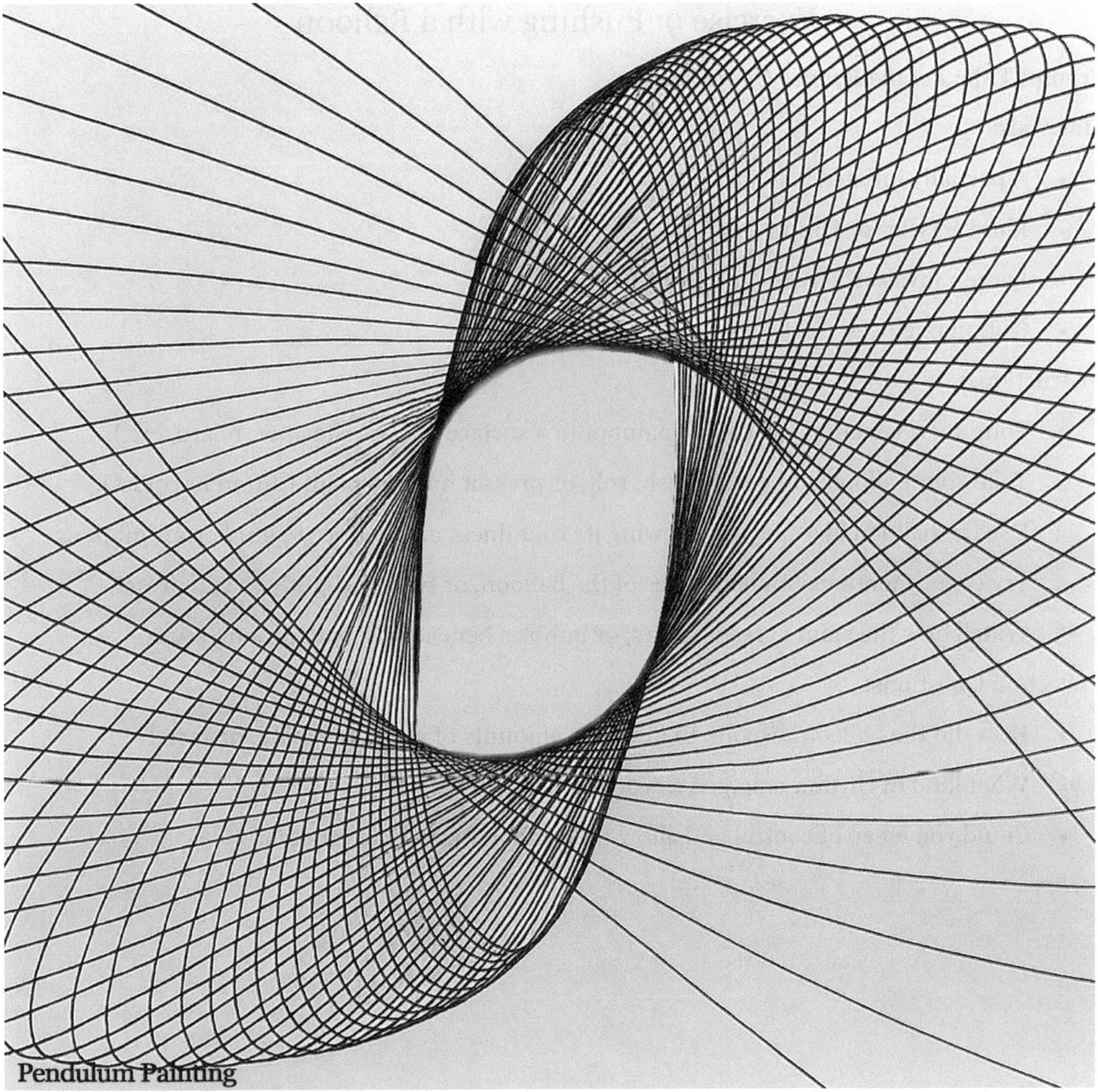

Pendulum Painting

Exercise 9: Pushing with a Balloon

Prompt Title: *Let the Bounce Guide You*

Materials:

- A partially inflated balloon
- Fluid acrylics or tempera paint
- Large canvas or paper
- Optional: gloves

Instructions:

1. Pour a few generous puddles of paint onto a surface (a canvas, paper, board, etc.).
2. Take your balloon and gently push, roll, or press it into the paint (different colors).
3. Use the balloon like a brush, allowing its roundness and bounce to guide your motions.
4. Try experimenting with both sides of the balloon, or twist it slightly as you press.
5. Watch how the paint spreads, blurs, or bubbles beneath the balloon's pressure.

Reflection Questions:

- How did the balloon respond to different amounts of paint, pressure, or speed?
- What kind of rhythm emerged as you worked?
- Could you let go of control and allow the balloon to lead the process?

Pushing with a Balloon

Exercise 11: Beating with a Tree Branch

Prompt Title: *Wild Marks, Honest Motion*

Materials:

- A flexible tree branch or stick
- Thick-bodied paint (e.g., acrylic)
- Canvas or heavy paper
- Protective sheet for splatter

Instructions:

1. Lay down your protective sheet and place your canvas or paper on a flat surface.
2. Dip the tip or full length of the tree branch into paint.
3. Beat, whip, drag, or snap the branch across the surface. Use your whole arm and vary your movement — sideways lashes, rhythmic taps, sudden jabs.
4. Let the raw texture of the branch leave its unpredictable imprint.
5. Pause and observe. Add more paint or shift your motion as it feels right.
6. Or simply add a moon — especially if the background invites it.

Reflection Questions:

- What energy did you bring to the surface — wildness, play, tension, or joy?
- How did it feel to let go of control and use your whole body?
- What kind of voice do these rough, spontaneous marks carry?

Beating with a Tree Branch

Exercise 12- No Plan, Just Play

Prompt Title: *Start Anywhere, Follow Everything*

Materials:

- Any kind of paint or mixed media
- Canvas, paper, or cardboard
- Brushes, sponges, fingers, or any tool that feels fun
- A willingness to explore

Instructions:

1. Begin with a completely blank surface and no plan.
2. Choose a color, tool, or shape that you're instinctively drawn to—and make the first mark.
3. Let that mark guide the next. Follow your curiosity rather than trying to "make something."
4. Switch colors or tools whenever you feel like it. Cover areas up. Repeat motions. Pause. Begin again.
5. Stop only when the piece feels like it's said something — even if you don't know what it is.

Reflection Questions:

- What came up emotionally as you created without a plan?
- Did you find any moments of rhythm, surprise, or resistance?
- How did it feel to play without needing a result?

No Plan, Just Play

Exercise 13- Free Rolling of Glass Marbles

Prompt Title: *Let Momentum Paint*

Materials:

- Several glass marbles (of same or different sizes) or small rolling balls
- Acrylic or tempera paint in different colors
- Cups or trays for dipping marbles
- A canvas or heavy paper (flat or slightly angled)
- Optional: gloves, palette knife, brushes

Instructions:

1. Dip the marbles into paint (black or different colors). Make sure they're well-coated.
2. Place them gently or drop them from a short height onto your canvas.
3. Tilt the canvas slowly to let gravity guide the marbles, or roll them by hand.
4. Let each marble carve its own path — spirals, zigzags, sudden stops.
5. Once dry, you can stop there — or respond.
6. After that you can add lines, highlights, create fingers, or paint with brushes.
7. Echo some trails, blur others. Follow what feels true.

Reflection Questions:

- How did it feel to give up control and let the marbles decide the flow?
- Were you tempted to guide them — or did you step back and watch?

What emotions did the unpredictable motion evoke?

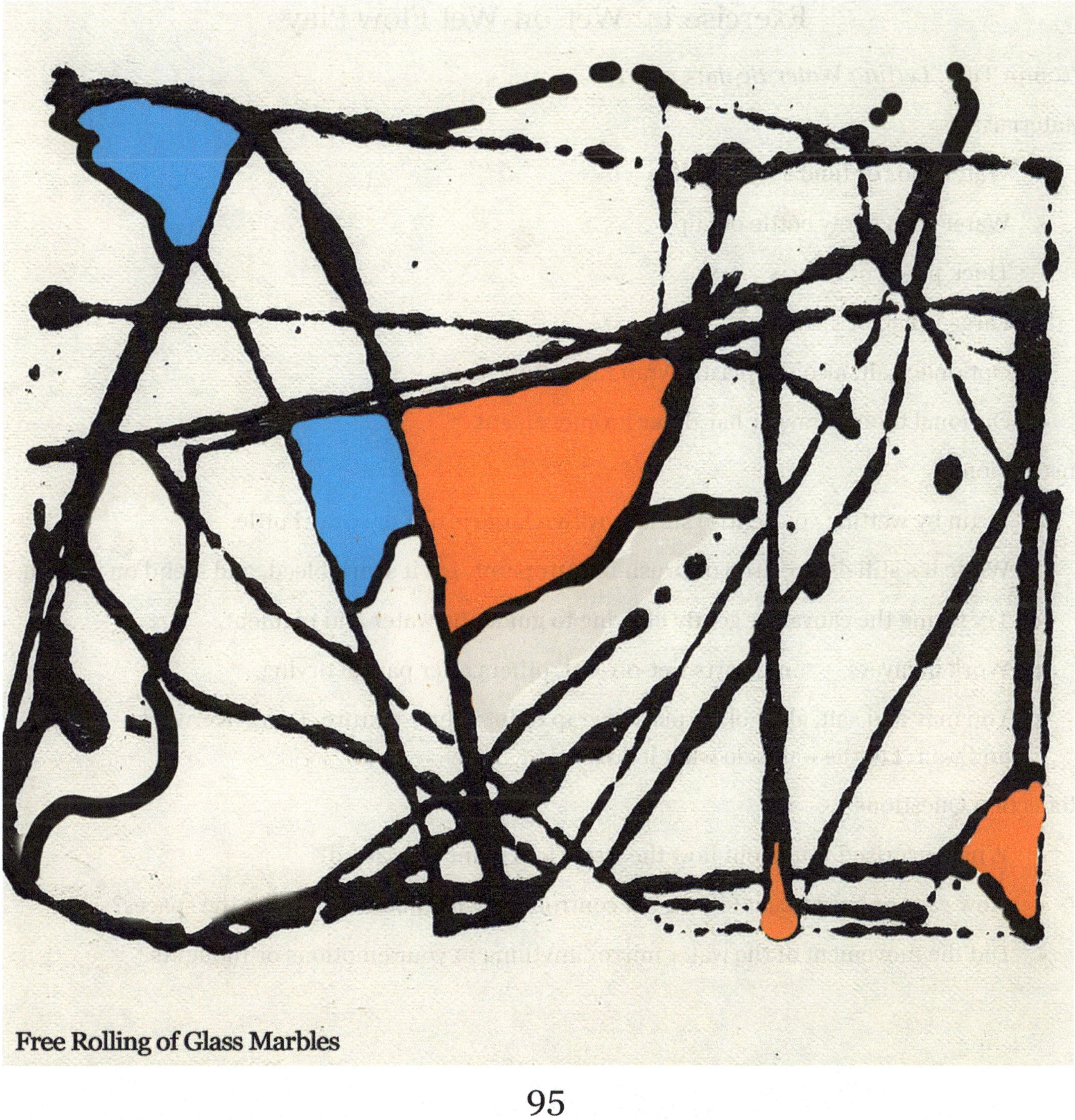

Free Rolling of Glass Marbles

Exercise 14: Wet-on-Wet Flow Play

Prompt Title: *Letting Water Be the Co-Artist*

Materials:

- Watercolor or fluid acrylic paints
- Water (in a spray bottle or cup)
- Thick paper or canvas
- Large brush or sponge
- Optional: salt, alcohol, plastic wrap for texture
- Optional tools: straw or hairdryer for movement

Instructions:

1. Begin by wetting your entire surface with a large brush or spray bottle.
2. While it's still damp, drop or brush in your paint. Let it swirl, bleed, and blend on its own.
3. Try tilting the canvas or gently blowing to guide the water and pigment.
4. Work in layers — some parts wet-on-wet, others after partial drying.
5. You may add salt, alcohol, or plastic wrap to introduce texture. Don't overwork — watch and wait. Let the water do what it does.

Reflection Questions:

- What surprised you about how the water and paint interacted?
- How easy or hard was it to let go of control and what about not filling the spaces?
- Did the movement of the water mirror anything in your emotions or thoughts?

Wet-on-Wet Flow Play

Exercise 15: Using Boll Chain

Prompt Title: *Trails of Tension and Grace*

Materials:

- A metal boll chain (or linked ball bearings)
- Fluid acrylics or ink
- Large canvas or thick paper
- Optional: gloves or tweezers for handling

Instructions:

1. Place rich spots or pools of paint directly onto your canvas. Use a variety of colors and arrange them freely across the surface.
2. Take the ball chain and gently drag it through the paint on the canvas. Vary the direction and speed depending on how the paint responds.
3. Experiment with different motions — sweeps, curves, wiggles, and sudden turns. You can drag the chain with your hand, or let parts of it drop and pull.
4. Notice how the chain creates bird feather– or flower petal–like imprints and layered trails as it picks up and deposits color.
5. Repeat as desired. Let each motion build a new layer. Pause to observe, then respond again.

Reflection Questions:

- How did the chain respond to motion — fluidly, unpredictably, or with resistance?
- Did allowing the tool to “lead” the motion change how you experienced the process?
- How did the balance between intention and accident shape your final piece?

Using Boll Chain

Exercise 16: The 5-Minute Daily Mark

Prompt Title: *Build a Ritual, Not a Result*

Materials:

- Any drawing or painting tool
- Paper, sketchbook, or canvas
- A timer (optional)

Instructions:

6. Set aside five minutes a day — no more, no less.
7. When the time comes, make your mark. Scribble. Smudge. Line. Dot. Fill the space — or don't.
8. Don't think about what to create. Just begin.
9. Let each day's mark respond to how you feel, what you hear, or what the moment holds.
10. Over time, observe how your visual language grows without pressure.

This exercise isn't about creating "art." It's about showing up — for yourself, your process, and your permission to explore. Let your mood guide you. Choose any background color that feels right in the moment.

Now that you've explored everything — here's how you can keep going, forever.
This is not an end, but a beginning.

Reflection Questions:

- What shifted in your energy before and after each session?
- Did the marks begin to tell a story over time?
- What did this ritual teach you about consistency, effort, or self-expression?

Minute Daily Mark

Part 7: Artwork Gallery

"Each piece holds a memory of motion."

Introductory Reflection

This gallery is a reflective chapter—
a place where images spoke without words.

The additional text is part of the process itself—
an invitation to dialogue.
Each artwork here still carries its own presence,
but now accompanied by a quiet voice:
a title and a few words that emerged along the way.

They do not aim to define.
They open a space.
A gesture toward meaning, not a conclusion.

These works are not polished performances,
but traces of honest movement—
guided by the rhythm of breath,
the curiosity of the hand,
and the quiet guidance of imagination.

Let these pages invite you to feel.
To pause.
To observe without the need to interpret.
To notice rhythm, tension, stillness, or flow.

Let your eyes wander.
Let your breath soften.
And gently remember:
This too is part of the process.

Traces of Time

Subtle layers, fading marks, aged texture

Like an old wall that's weathered a thousand quiet days,
this piece carries the silence of time lived through.
Its softness invites you to listen—
not to a story told aloud,
but to one whispered through absence,
through what remains after letting go.

There is no urgency here.
Just the slow drift of memory settling into form.
A surface that has been touched,
and touched again,
until even the marks begin to forget why they were made.

Notice how some lines cling while others fade.
How warmth and erosion coexist.
How even stillness can speak.

Let this be a place to pause.
Not to remember, but simply to be.
To be with time, as it is now.
Still passing. Still painting.

Traces of Time

Marks of Letting Go

Wild strokes, chaotic releases, spontaneous energy

There are moments when control dissolves—
and what spills out is raw,
unfiltered, unplanned.

These strokes don't ask for precision.
They don't follow rules,
and they certainly don't wait for permission.

Red, blue, yellow—each color strikes
as if pushed by a burst of feeling,
by a memory,
or by the need to breathe.

This is not a mess.
It is movement.
It is honesty.

Each arc a gesture of surrender.
Each mark a release from the grip of overthinking.
Nothing to fix, nothing to frame—
just motion turned visible.

Let your own hand follow.
Let the energy move through you.
And notice:
letting go leaves beautiful traces.

Marks of Letting Go

Flow

Fluid motion, organic shapes

This painting moves like a breath—soft, seamless, and alive.
It invites no urgency, no sharpness—only the gentle permission to melt.
Colors drift and blend like thoughts without borders,
as if each curve remembers where it came from,
yet feels no need to return.

There is no beginning and no end—only motion becoming form.
In its stillness, a quiet current continues beneath.
This is not a shape to be understood, but a feeling to rest in.
A visual exhale.
A reminder that everything can shift
without losing its essence.

Flow

Contrast

Bold oppositions of light/dark or texture/smooth

This piece doesn't whisper.
It declares—through every sharp turn and sudden shift.
Black and white collide without apology.
Edges are not softened, but carved.
Tension breathes in every bold stroke.

Yet even in this starkness, balance holds its ground.
The orange—unexpected and raw—
erupts like a heartbeat in a room of silence.
There is rhythm in resistance,
beauty in what doesn't blend.

This is the language of opposites,
where clarity lives not in harmony,
but in the fearless coexistence of extremes.

Contrast

Rhythm

Repeating motifs, patterned movement

Circles pulse like quiet drums.
Each ring repeats a memory—
not identical, but familiar,
like the echo of footsteps on a well-worn path.

There's order here,
but not rigidity.
The rhythm flows in waves,
inviting the eye to dance
from one form to the next,
finding rest in repetition
and energy in return.

This is not stillness.
It is motion held in form—
a quiet beat drawn on canvas.
Steady. Measured. Alive.

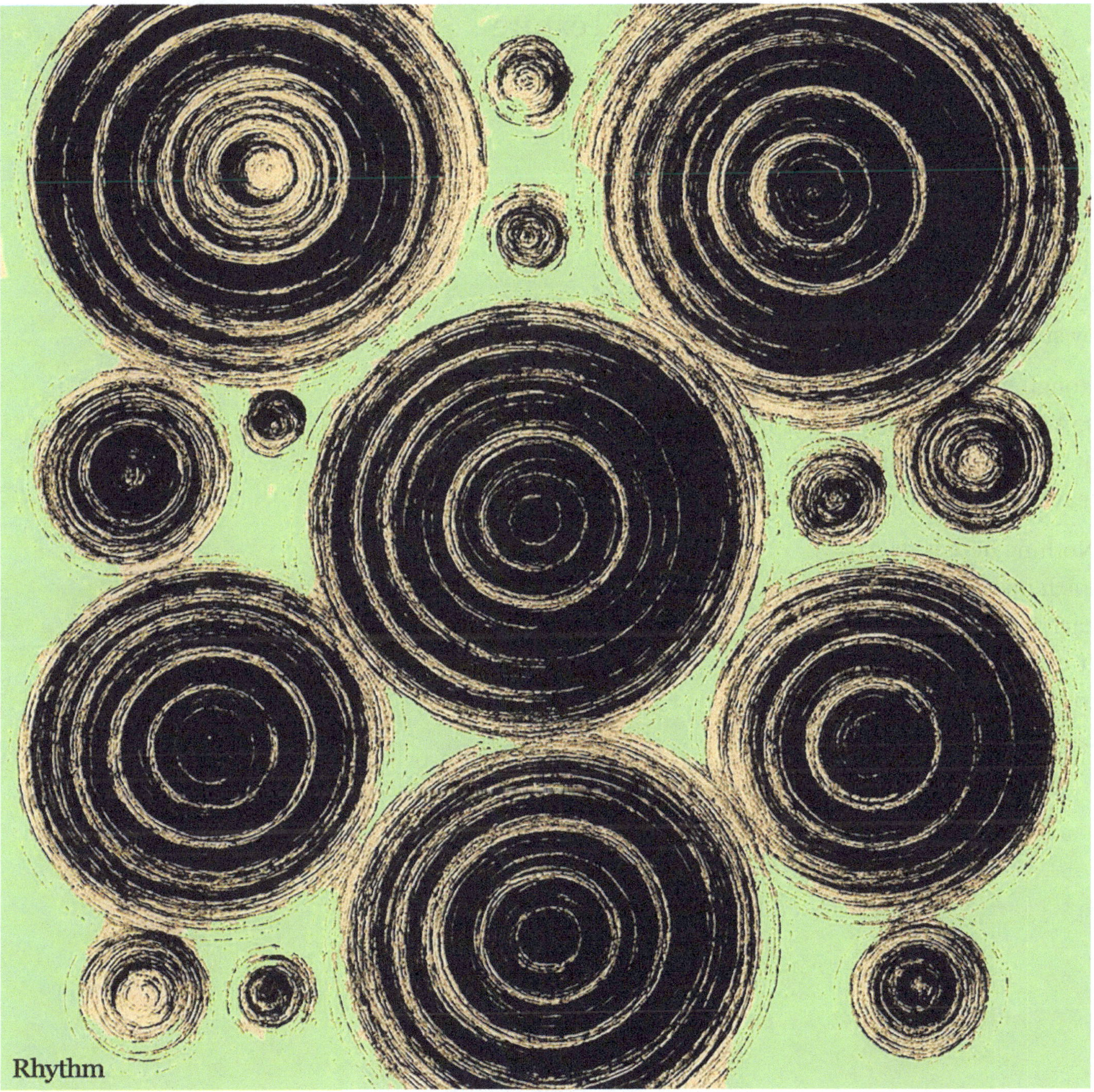

Rhythm

Texture

Built-up surfaces, tactile visual elements

This is where the eye wants to touch—
where sight leans into feeling.

The surface rises and sinks
like land shaped by time,
by weather, by pressure,
by stories pressed into place.

Rough meets smooth,
soft bleeds into sharp,
and the unseen fingers of the past
leave trails in the present moment.

Nothing here is flat.
Each mark has weight,
each layer has memory.
It invites you to pause,
to not just look—
but to listen through your skin.

Texture

Silence

Minimal marks, open space, contemplative mood

There is power in restraint—
a whisper held in golden air.

This space does not beg for more.
It offers less
so you can feel more.

A single curve,
soft and sure,
draws the breath inward.
Not to speak—
but to notice.

It is not absence,
but presence distilled—
like still water
holding the sky.

Here, silence is not empty.
It is full
of everything
you finally have room to hear.

Silence

Inner Image

A dance between intuition and silence

At the center, a warmth—
not seen,
but remembered.

Colors move not outward,
but inward—
pulling the gaze
into the hush of knowing.

It is not painted with reason.
It arrives
from stillness,
from the place where feeling
finds form
before words do.

This is the image
that was always there—
just waiting
for your silence
to become
a listening.

Inner Image

Part 8: Looking Back and Moving Forward

"Every end is a beginning in disguise."

Final word

As we reach the end of this journey through Process Art, it's important to pause — not to finish, but to reflect on how every beginning leads us to a new path of exploration.

You've encountered materials, methods, and moments that encourage letting go of expectations. You've been invited to drip, splash, pull, push, feel, and even fail — with purpose. What you've read and practiced here is just a glimpse into what Process Art can become in your own hands. These exercises are not rules — they're doors. And behind each one is a unique form of discovery only *you* can make.

The final work, in truth, is not a canvas or paper. It's you—the artist becoming more yourself, more aware, more free. You've seen how a single gesture can carry emotion, how a mistake can transform into meaning, and how silence can guide your hand more clearly than thought.

As you continue beyond this book, remember: Process Art is not a chapter you close — it's a living method. Keep creating. Keep noticing. Keep letting your process unfold, without judgment and without destination. That's where the real art lives.

About the Author

David Omidvar is a multidisciplinary creator — painter, photographer, and author — with a background in engineering and a lifelong passion for artistic exploration. His creative path blends curiosity, emotional depth, and a hands-on approach to intuitive expression. These have been the guiding lights of his artistic journey for more than three decades.

Guided by the values of presence, process, and personal growth, David approaches art not as performance, but as practice. Whether through vivid canvases, evocative photography, or reflective writing, his work invites others to trust their instincts, embrace imperfection, and find joy in the act of making.

Through his books, he encourages readers to release expectations, follow their inner rhythm, and experience the transformative power of creativity.

This book on Process Art is part of a growing legacy — a tribute to flow, freedom, discovery, and expression without limits. It marks the beginning of what may become a broader Art Exploration series.

Thank you for being part of the journey.
– David Omidvar

The next page is not empty —

it’s the beginning of your journey.

An open path toward the creativity

you haven’t yet expressed.

Made in the USA
Las Vegas, NV
22 September 2025

27637026R00070